D1631522

UGANDA RWENZORI

A Range of Images

Dedicated to Bernard Muganda,
my teacher in Africa.

UGANDA RWENZORI

A Range of Images

David Pluth

with historical photographs by Vittorio Sella

'… it felt as though we had emerged from a world of fantasy,
where nothing was real but only a wild and lovely flight of
imagination. I think perhaps the range is unique.
It is well named Mountains of the Moon.'

Eric Shipton, *Upon that Mountain*

Little Wolf Press

ACKNOWLEDGEMENTS

I would like to thank the many people who have helped me with their encouragement, ideas and their time: Mirjam Blaak and staff at Delmira Travel in Kampala; my wife Patricia for wading through more than just the Rwenzori with me; Rwenzori Mountaineering Services; my porters, guides and friends in the Rwenzori, Ezra, Jerome, Julius, Joel, Semeon and Vincent; my over-worked assistant Israel Byaruhanga; John and Adeerie Simpson of Kijura Tea Company in Fort Portal; Captain Mark Price of Ndali Lodge; the Alvigini family of Biella, Italy; Stephen Kitching who tried to teach me about tea; and Mr and Mrs Guy Yeoman, who have kindly been enthusiastic about answering my questions.

Finally, I would like to extend a special thanks to the Istituto di Fotografia Alpina 'Vittorio Sella', and the Sella Foundation of Biella, Italy, for their co-operation in permitting me to use photographs from the 1906 Duke of Abruzzi expedition to the Rwenzori which were printed for this book from the original negatives of Vittorio Sella.

Copyright © 1996 David William Pluth

The right of David William Pluth to be identified as the author of the work has been asserted by him in accordance with the Copyright, Designs and Patents Act 1988.

First published 1996 by

Little Wolf Press
Dorfhalde 10   Tel ++41 (1) 926 14 07
CH-8712 Staefa   Fax ++41 (1) 926 17 44
Switzerland   Net Coyotech@msn.com

All rights reserved. No part of this publication may be reproduced, stored in a retrieval system or transmitted in any form or by any means, electronic, mechanical, photocopying, recording or otherwise without the prior written permission of the copyright holder for which application should be addressed in the first instance to the publisher. No liability shall be attached to the author, the copyright holder or the publisher for loss or damage of any nature suffered as a result of reliance on the reproduction of any of the contents of this publication or any errors or omissions in its contents.

A catalogue record for this book is available from the Schweizerische Landesbibliothek and from the British Library.

ISBN 3-906745-00-7

All photographs taken by David Pluth unless otherwise stated.

Designed by Peter Dolton
Produced by Book Production Consultants plc, Cambridge, England
Colour reproduction by EAE, Norwich, England
Printed by Kyodo Printing Co (S'pore) Pte Ltd

CONTENTS

AUTHOR'S NOTE

This is a book of pictures, of images and personal impressions of the Uganda Rwenzori mountains, the compact, jagged range famous in history as the mysterious 'Mountains of the Moon', the snow-covered equatorial African peaks that feed the waters of the Nile. The images convey my personal feelings of the mountains, foothills, towns and people of the Uganda Rwenzori as they exist today. Like all picture books, this is a snapshot in time. It shows some things that are amusing, some things that are sad, some things that have remained and probably will remain unchanged for centuries, and some things that will have changed by the time this book is published. My intent is to record impressions. Life moves on, the picture stands still.

The definitive photographs of the Rwenzori mountains in their wild state were taken during the Duke of Abruzzi's expedition in 1906 by Vittorio Sella, one of the greatest of all alpine photographers. Rather than trying to duplicate his work, which would be an impossible task in both logistical and artistic terms, I have chosen to include some of his photographs in this book.

The spelling of place names in this book is that which is popularly accepted or used on current maps. Thus, I use Rwenzori and not Ruwenzori, the spelling which was favoured by Stanley and subsequently perpetuated in the literature, *except* where I quote directly

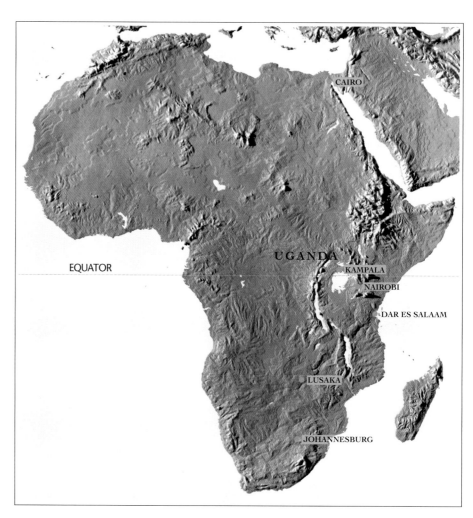

from historical sources. Further, Rwenzori is used as both singular and plural, so we have 'in the Rwenzori' rather than 'in the Rwenzoris'.

Heights and distances are given accurately in metres and kilometres and approximately in feet and miles.

The photographs in this book were taken by the author using either a Hasselblad 503cx square format camera or a Canon EOS-5 35mm camera.

David Pluth

INTRODUCTION

LITTLE MORE THAN one hundred years ago there had been no reliable sighting of the Rwenzori mountains reported to the geographical societies of Europe and America. While the mountains were rumoured – and believed – to have existed since the time of Ptolemy, their location was not firmly drawn on a dependable map by someone who had been there, seen them and reported back to their home country. The local inhabitants, of course, knew where the peaks were all along, but that knowledge somehow was not officially absorbed. Today, Uganda receives more than 100,000 tourists each year and the number is growing rapidly. Wide-body jets land at the sleek Entebbe

Jerry can seller in Kampala

airport on the shores of Lake Victoria, near the bustling city of Kampala with its fine hotels, casinos and rush hour traffic jams, and disgorge trekking groups outfitted with bulky boots, ice axes, ski poles, crampons, guidebooks, multiple sets of maps and detailed itineraries of exactly where each day and night will be spent in Uganda. If a group arrives in the morning, they can be at the base of the mountains, 400 kilometres away, by early evening. A few days later, if the weather co-operates, they can be standing on the summit of Mount Stanley, the highest peak in the range and the third highest mountain in Africa. Contrast that to the years and months of tortuous travel endured by the early explorers like Stanley himself, Gessi, Speke, Baker, Emin and others, wandering through central Africa, most of whom never saw the mountains at all. Now the Rwenzori, the almost unknown mountains, are a major tourist destination, National Park and United Nations World Heritage Site.

Ever since they became widely known outside Uganda, the Rwenzori have been

changing. Nowadays, the most visible, and probably preventable, changes in the Rwenzori are to the fragile vegetation along the heavily travelled tracks; tourism is simply loving it to death. Nor have the villages and cultures of the region remained immune as political stability, population growth, tourism and the first signs of economic prosperity begin to push further into the mountains, prompting the clearing of higher and steeper slopes for farmland, subtly altering the way people live and – call it what you will, decay or progress – the way people want to live. There is a continuing need to plan for an always changing and uncertain future.

Terrace of the Speke Hotel, Kampala

Kampala merchant

THE LANDSCAPE

The Rwenzori mountains straddle the equator along the border between eastern Zaire and western Uganda, extending north–south for about 100 kilometres (60 miles) and east–west for about 50 kilometres (30 miles). Six peaks at the centre of the range are over 4,570 metres (15,000 feet), with the highest point being the glaciated Margherita Peak on Mount Stanley at 5,109 metres (16,763 feet). The snow-covered part of the range, comprising the tallest peaks, extends for only about 18 kilometres (11 miles). Rising gradually from the highland plains of Uganda, the mountains fall steeply on the west to the rift valley of the Semliki river, western source of the Nile. At the southern end of the range lies Lake Edward and at the northern, Lake Albert. Most of the range is today within the boundaries of Uganda's Rwenzori National Park; the western flanks are part of Zaire's Virunga National Park.

Essentially, due to the uniform distribution of rainfall throughout the year, the high humidity and the efficiency of the vegetation in water catchment and retention, the Rwenzori mountains should be regarded as a vast elevated wetland and water reservoir.

The upper elevations of the range are often covered in cloud by day, resulting in an extremely humid climate with up to 50 centimetres (20 inches) of rain during the wettest month, November. At this time of year the rivers can turn to raging torrents, and have cut deep valleys in the outer spurs of the range. The trails become rivers of mud and the alpine bogs can seem bottomless to the struggling trekker. From the central peaks of Stanley, Speke and Baker the main branches of the Mubuku river descend to the east, while on the west the four principal streams

unite in the Semliki river. As the ancient geographers had guessed, the snows and rivers of the Rwenzori mountains do indeed feed the headwaters of the Nile.

Geologically the mountains are young, created less than 10 million years ago by an upthrust from faults in the neighbouring rift valley. Unlike Kilimanjaro and Mount Kenya, the Rwenzori are not volcanic but predominantly old quartzite and gneiss. The combination of sharp upthrust and hard rock give the Rwenzori its jagged alpine character. While the mountains themselves are not volcanic in origin, the eastern foothills are dotted with gem-like

Freshfield Pass

lakes within volcanic craters. To the south are the Mfumbiro volcanoes surrounded by lava-covered ground and many crater lakes.

The glaciers of the range are small and receding. They have no real basins, but instead resemble ice-caps. None of the glaciers descend lower than 4,250 metres (about 14,000 feet). Many of the small lakes are the remnants of former glaciers. Glacial streams descending from the mountains generally are small, fast-flowing and clean, carrying little detritus

from the slow-moving glaciers. Due to its great extent and height, the range acts as a large condenser drawing up hot moist air from the surrounding plains and precipitating it as snow, rain and mist. Despite the small size of the streams, their sheer number discharge a tremendous volume of water to feed the White Nile.

The climate is wet. The Rwenzori have two annual rainy seasons: from mid-March to May and from September to mid-December. Rainfall varies with altitude, reaching up to 2,000–3,000 millimetres per year and is heaviest on the eastern slopes facing the prevailing winds.

There are dry seasons, usually from June to August and mid-December to mid-March, but even then there can be periods of sustained rainfall. Trekkers should therefore be prepared for heavy rain at any time of the year, even during the dry seasons, which can sometimes be more theoretical than real.

The mountains may be shrouded in mist at all times of the year, sometimes for weeks. It is these mists which create the characteristic rime ice formations on the higher ridges. The best weather each day is likely to be from about 0200 hours to 0700 hours, in other words at night. Successful climbers will have kept this in mind and started early.

There are animals, but very few large ones, in part due to heavy hunting during the 1970s and 1980s. In the forest zones elephant and buffalo might still be seen, but rarely. Chimpanzees, blue monkeys and Rwenzori colobus monkeys are more often in evidence, as well as duiker, forest hog and leopard which sometimes wander up to 4,000 metres. Shrews and voles can be found at all elevations, while hyrax prefer higher living.

The distribution of the luxuriant Rwenzori flora is controlled largely by altitude, although plants normally found at lower elevations may also grow in sheltered high valleys. At higher altitudes some plants reach an unusually large size, such as the lobelia and giant groundsels, possibly the result of great daily temperature variation and lack of seasons.

Approximately, the overlapping vegetation zones are:

– 1,000 to 2,100 metres. The inhabited foothill zone and generally cultivated with bananas, coffee, cassava, millet, beans and sweet potatoes. This zone of fire-induced poor quality grassland is subject to soil erosion and reduced fertility.

– 2,100 to 2,400 metres. The montane forest zone of mixed broad-leaved and podocarpus montane rain forest. Trees rarely exceed 30 metres and the forest canopy is broken, allowing a dense underbrush to grow. Common trees include symphonia, a tall tree with red flowers seen in the lower Mubuku valley, podocarpus (podo), a tall conifer with narrow dark leaves found around Nyabitaba Hut, giant tree ferns up to 5 metres tall, wild banana, with large leaves and short trunks, impatiens, with small pink or white flowers, found by streams, white begonias, bracken fern, ballflower and hibiscus.

– 2,400 to 3,000 metres. Bamboo grows on the gentler slopes while giant tree heathers are found on the open ridge tops, sometimes reaching a height of 10 metres. A few giant lobelia are found, while a dense tangled cover can be formed by the flowering mimulopsis elliotii.

– 3,000 to 3,800 metres. The ridge tops and areas of poor soil are often covered with giant heathers draped with long strands of usnea (old man's beard), a pale yellow-green lichen. On the ground, deep moss blankets the complex root systems of the trees. East African rosewood with its masses of reddish flowers, the tree groundsel (senecio) and giant lobelia are common. Species of everlasting flowers (helichrysum) are common and the bogs are covered with giant tussocks surrounded with moss, liverworts and lichens.

– 3,800 to 4,500 metres. This is the alpine zone, with white-flowered everlastings growing in thickets and tussock grasses covering the bogs. Climax forms of afro-alpine gigantism are shown in the commonly found senecio (giant groundsels) and distinctive lobelia which have been described as 'Africa's botanical big game'.

Lobelia rosette

A BIT OF HISTORY

For centuries, legend and rumour had told of the existence of snowy mountains that fed the Nile. About 1800 years ago, Ptolemy showed them on a map and called them the Lunae Montes, the Mountains of the Moon. Taking Ptolemy's map as their basis, cartographers through the centuries depicted conjectural mountains and lakes on their charts of Africa, but the precise identification of Kilimanjaro, Mount Kenya, Lake Victoria and the Rwenzori range did not occur until the middle to late 1800s. For many years there was some competition (and, in some circles, it continues today) among explorers about which snow-covered African peaks fit the title Mountains of the Moon. In 1848 Johann Rebmann was the first European to record sighting snow in the tropics when he saw Mount Kilimanjaro. The next year his colleague Johann Lewis Krapf sighted Mount Kenya, but it was soon shown that neither Kilimanjaro nor Mount Kenya had any connection with the Nile, hence were not the true Mountains of the Moon. John Hanning Speke, on his successful 1861 Nile search expedition, circuiting to the west of Lake Victoria, looked further to the west and writes in his *Source of the Nile* that he saw 'in the distance some bold sky-scraping cones … The Mfumbiro cones in Ruanda, which I believe to reach 10,000 feet, are said to be the highest of the Mountains of the Moon.' These are the Virunga mountains, a group of volcanoes about 150 kilometres south of the Rwenzori. But it was Sir Henry Morton Stanley's claim to have found the Mountains of the Moon which has best stood the tests of time and popular acceptance.

Stanley made the first well documented sighting of the Rwenzori by a European in 1876, but his view was not clear, nor is it likely that he really understood what he was seeing, having been told it was the 'great mountain of Gambaragara'. Throughout the 1870s and early 1880s other European travellers such as Baker, Emin and Gessi passed close enough to the Rwenzori to have seen the mountains, but failed to do so because of the prevailing clouds and mist blocking their view.

Stanley seems to have had a small obsession about finding the Mountains of the Moon. He had the name ready – Ruwenzori (as he spelled it), a Bantu word, or rather a collection of Bantu sounds, interpreted as 'hill of rains', and he just had to find a suitable mountain to which to attach it. That none of the local people called the mountains Ruwenzori did not seem to matter to Stanley; once he found the mountains he ensured the popularity of the name through his books and lectures. In 1887 he embarked with an expeditionary force sent by Britain to rescue Emin Pasha. The expedition was camped on the western escarpment above Lake Albert for several months and had not sighted the mountains. On 20 April 1888 Stanley asked his medical officer, Thomas Heazle Parke, together with another of his officers, A.J. Mounteney Jephson, to take the expedition's boat from the high camp down to the lake to be launched. Parke later wrote, 'On the march we distinctly saw snow on the top of a huge mountain situated to the south-west of our position. As this was a curious and unexpected sight we halted the caravan to have a good view.' Parke reported his sighting to Stanley two days later, but Stanley, never one to let someone else stand in the spotlight, dismissed Parke by claiming that he must have seen some lower hills in a different direction, certainly not the mighty Ruwenzori. Nevertheless, a month later, on 24 May 1888, Stanley himself clearly saw the mountains and the snows. He wrote, 'My eyes were directed by a boy to a mountain, said to be covered with salt, and I saw a peculiar shaped cloud of a most beautiful silver colour, which assumed the proportions and appearance of a vast mountain covered with snow. Following its form downward, I became struck with the deep blue-black colour of its base, and wondered if it portended another tornado; then, as the sight descended to the gap between the eastern and western plateaus, I became for the first time conscious that what I gazed upon was not the image or semblance of a vast mountain, but the solid substance of a real one, with its summit covered with snow … It now

dawned upon me that this must be the Ruwenzori …'

The following year, 1889, Stanley returned to the Rwenzori with Emin Pasha and travelled south along the western slope of the range, around the southern end, then, turned north and followed the eastern, Ugandan, slopes. He spent more than three months from April to July in the foothills and saw the snowy peaks often. To gain more information about the

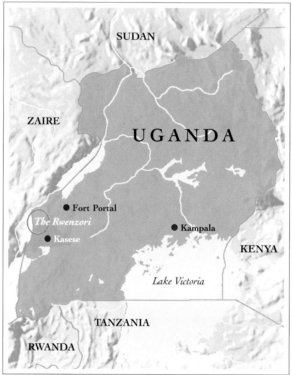

mountains he asked for volunteers amongst his party, thoroughly ragged after two and a half years of travel, 'to win immortal renown by scaling the heights of the famous Mountains of the Moon', but nearly everyone was too exhausted or sick with fever to show any enthusiasm for the idea. Stanley himself said, 'My strength was so far recovered that I could walk 200 yards.' But one man, Lieutenant W.G. Stairs, 'took a sly look' at the peaks and said, 'I'll go, like a shot'. Stairs climbed to over 3,000 metres towards Mount Emin, the first real attempt to climb the

mountains, even though he remained within the vegetated zone.

In 1891 Emin Pasha visited the Semliki river with Dr Franz Stuhlmann, who led a five-day trip up one of the western valleys into the heart of the Rwenzori reaching Kampi ya Chupa (Camp of the Bottle). It was Dr Stuhlmann who recognised that the Rwenzori was not a single mountain but a range, and it was he who first described accurately the successive zones of vegetation from the foothills to the snowline. Four years later, in 1895, the naturalist G.F. Scott Elliot made several visits to the mountains from the west and was the first to find a route from the east up the Mubuku valley, part of the current popular tourist circuit. Scott Elliot reached his greatest altitude, about 4,200 metres (about 13,800 feet) in the Butagu valley.

At the end of the nineteenth century Uganda was gradually being brought under British colonial administration, a time of great turmoil in the country. Following Scott Elliot's expeditions, very little exploration was done in the Rwenzori until 1900, when J.E.S. Moore ascended the Mubuku valley, becoming the first person to reach the glaciers at its head, climbing to an altitude of about 4,540 metres (about 14,900 feet) on Mount Baker. The route up the Mubuku valley was becoming well known – three other parties ascended the Mubuku in 1900 and another the following year. In 1904 Dr J.J. David, a Swiss geologist, finally reached the Stanley plateau from the Zaire side, but exactly where is not clear.

With the rise of colonial administration and increased security within the country, the transport problems that had plagued the early European explorers and travellers in Uganda were partially relieved. On 21 December 1901 the last spike in the last rail of the Uganda Railway was driven, completing a line from Mombasa on the Kenyan coast to Kisumu (Port Florence) on the east side of Lake Victoria. Although the railway did not actually reach Uganda until 1928, lake steamers ran from the Kisumu railhead to Entebbe on the north-west shore. It was now possible to travel nearly to the centre of the African continent quickly, safely and in relative comfort. Shortly after the railway began operating, the period 1905–1906 saw one of the most intense concentrations of exploration and scientific interest in the Rwenzori, before or since.

In 1905, true mountaineers came to the Rwenzori for the first time. Douglas Freshfield and A.L. Mumm, with the guide Moritz Inderbinnen of Zermatt, went up the Mubuku valley and reached the snows but were prevented from going further by the continuous rainfall, a feature well-known to present-day travellers in the Rwenzori. In 1906 expeditions up the Mubuku valley were made by the Rev A.B. Fisher and his wife (their second trip), and by the Austrian mountaineer R. Grauer and two English missionaries, H.E. Maddox and the Rev H.W. Tegart (also their second trip). Grauer's party made the first ascent of any of the Rwenzori peaks, now Grauer's Rock on Mount Baker. In late 1905 the British Museum had sent out A.F.R. Wollaston, an experienced mountaineer, and H.B. Woosnam to study the flora and fauna; in February 1906 they made the first ascent of Wollaston Peak on Mount Baker, 4,659 metres (15,286 feet) and the second ascent of Grauer's Rock.

The exploration excitement of these times culminated in 1906 with one of the most well-equipped and thoughtfully planned expeditions ever to enter the Rwenzori, mounted by Prince Luigi Amadeo di Savoia, the Duke of Abruzzi. This powerful expedition was composed of six scientists, four alpine guides from Courmayeur and a photographer, Vittorio Sella. Over 300 porters were employed. Based at Bujongolo, they ascended and named most of the major peaks, returned with volumes of scientific data, and prepared an excellent map and photographs of the mountains.

It was not until 1926, 20 years after the Duke of Abruzzi's expedition, that the highest peaks of the Rwenzori were climbed again, this time by the much smaller expedition led by Dr G. Noel Humphries, who had made the first ascent of the volcano Popocatépetl in Mexico and who was later to take on Mount Everest. He was also the first person to take aerial photographs of the Rwenzori range. Humphries made seven expeditions to the mountains between 1926 and 1932, adding greatly to the knowledge about the Rwenzori.

The third successful ascent of Mount Stanley was made in 1932 by the famous British mountaineers and explorers Eric Shipton and H.W. Tilman, early true believers in the modern alpine concept of 'fast, light and dry'. They spent 16 days in the range, based under a wet rock overhang by the side of Lake Bujuku and ascended Mounts Speke, Stanley and Baker. This last was climbed by a strenuous one-day effort ascending the north-west face to the ridge, traversing to the summit, descending by a route unknown to them toward Freshfield Pass, down to the Kitandara Lakes, climbing up to Scott Elliot Pass and then descending again to their rock shelter at Lake Bujuku. The next day they broke camp and double-marched out to the roadhead.

In 1932 a major Belgian scientific expedition based at Kiondo was of great importance in the exploration and study of the western (Zairean) side, of the Stanley group. Under the leadership of the Count de Grünne, this expedition was accompanied by Swiss guides and more than 500 porters. They made the fourth ascent of Mount Stanley, the first time it was climbed from the west side.

In the early years of the Uganda Mountain Club, Henry Osmaston was influential in the study of the range, publishing, with David Pasteur, his excellent *Guide to the Ruwenzori* in 1972. In recent years Guy Yeoman has contributed to the future development and protection of the Rwenzori mountains by working tirelessly for the establishment of a National Park. One of the newer huts on the central circuit has been named in his honour. Another man of distinction, who also has a trail hut named after him, is John Matte, a Konzo who was the Uganda Mountain Club agent and later chairman of Rwenzori Mountaineering Services. It was he perhaps more than anyone else who kept alive the traditions of the guides and porters during Uganda's difficult years and was instrumental in maintaining interest in the region.

WHY IS IT CALLED …?

The highest peak of the Rwenzori range is now known as Mount Stanley, with its three summits Albert, Alexandra and Margherita (the highest). Previously the mountain was known variously as Semper, Kanjangungwe, Ingomwimbi and Duwoni, names it sometimes shared with Mount Baker, which was also known as Weismann, Moebius, Kanyangogwe and Kiyanje! Henry Stanley himself called the peak Saddle Mountain – or was he really referring to Mount Gessi? The Duke of Abruzzi, following his ascent, named the mountain 'Stanley', the highest summit 'Margherita' after Queen Margherita of Italy and the second summit 'Alexandra' after the British Queen, wife of King Edward VII. The third peak he ignored, considering it only a subsidiary spur. Following its first ascent in 1932 by the de Grünne expedition it was named after King Albert of Belgium, a man who loved mountains.

When the Duke of Abruzzi mapped the Rwenzori in 1906, consistent with the fashion of his time, he gained the privilege to re-name the peaks (which in fact was necessary to clear up the existing confusion). Rather than using local names, the Duke called the six highest peaks after significant European explorers of the region including, at the behest of the British Royal Geographic Society, himself. So now we have Mounts Baker, Speke, Gessi, Emin, Stanley and Luigi di Savoia (after the Duke of Abruzzi), which settled the issue of names. But who were the people behind these names? What did they do? In every instance they were accomplished, complex individuals who lived fascinating, often difficult, lives and sometimes met a violent end.

John Hanning Speke (1827–1864) joined an expedition to explore Somaliland led by the linguist, diplomat and writer Sir Richard Burton in 1854. They were lucky to survive the trip, but only two years later, in 1856, they set out together again on an expedition sponsored by the Royal Geographical Society to search for the great East African equatorial lakes that were believed to exist and thought to be the sources of the Nile. They found Lake Tanganyika in 1858. When Burton became too ill to travel, Speke set out alone and became the first European to sight Lake Victoria, which he believed was the source of the Nile, even though this was hotly disputed by Burton. On a later expedition in 1862 with James Augustus Grant, Speke discovered Ripon Falls and descended the Nile as far as Juba, meeting Sir Samuel Baker and his wife, who were ascending the river. Despite his observations and beliefs, Speke never proved conclusively that Lake Victoria was the source of the Nile, and the day before he was to debate the subject publicly against Burton, a forceful and convincing speaker, Speke died in a shooting accident that many, including Burton, suspected was suicide.

Sir Samuel White Baker (1821–1893), a wealthy and prodigiously strong Scotsman, was the first European to sight Lake Albert just north of the Rwenzori. He also discovered Murchison Falls. After a long period in Mauritius and Ceylon, in 1861 he set out from Cairo to search for the source of the Nile with his beautiful and capable wife, a Transylvanian girl he had purchased at a slave bazaar in the Balkans. In 1862 they proceeded up the Nile to Juba, where they met the British explorers John Hanning Speke and James Augustus Grant. Informed by Speke of a lake said to be crossed by the Nile on its course to Juba, the Bakers continued upriver and, on 14 March 1864, reached the lake and named it Albert, in honour of Queen Victoria's husband, who had died in 1861. From 1869 to 1873 Baker commanded an expedition on behalf of the Ottoman Viceroy of Egypt to suppress slavery and open trade in the equatorial lake region, and never saw the Rwenzori.

Romulo Gessi (1831–1881) was an Italian military officer who in 1874 joined the administration of General Charles Gordon in the Equatoria Province of Egyptian Sudan and made the first circumnavigation of Lake Albert to the north of the Rwenzori. Remarkably, he did not see the mountains. Later, he became the Governor of Bhar-el-Ghazal Province, with the rank of Pasha. Though relatively obscure, he is considered to be one of the greatest Italian explorers on the Nile, a person for whom the tough and disciplined Gordon had utmost respect. In 1881 he was recalled from Bhar-el-Ghazal by the Egyptian government and was blocked for three months in the Sudd swamps of the Nile. Most of the 400 men in his party died of starvation and Gessi himself succumbed only two days after finally reaching Egypt.

Mohammed Emin Pasha (1840–1892), originally Eduard Schnitzer, was a Prussian doctor who had been tutor to the children of a Turkish pasha, had an affair with their mother, and, after his employer's death, became head of the family. Leaving them all behind in 1875, he journeyed to Cairo where he was appointed medical officer in the Egyptian army under General Charles Gordon, who named him governor of Equatoria Province in Sudan in 1878. In that capacity Emin Pasha made explorations of eastern Sudan and central Africa that contributed greatly to the geographical and scientific knowledge of the region. In 1883 a revolt broke out in Sudan under the leadership of the Mahdi; the Egyptian government abandoned the province in the following year and Emin Pasha found himself isolated by the rebel forces. In April 1888 he was rescued by Sir Henry Morton Stanley who tried in vain to persuade him to return to Egypt. In a second Mahdist revolt later that year, Emin Pasha was deposed and imprisoned. After his release he returned to Egypt and resigned his office. In 1890 he was commissioned by the German East Africa Company to lead an expedition into the regions of central Africa claimed by Germany. He was murdered by Arab slave traders in October 1892, at Kanema, in the Congo (now Zaire).

Sir Henry Morton Stanley (1841–1904), whether he actually said it or not, will always be remembered for the phrase, 'Dr Livingston, I presume?' Controversial yet popular, Stanley was an Anglo-American journalist and a leading figure in the exploration and colonisation of Africa. Born in Wales as John Rowlands, he sailed at the age of 18 to New Orleans, where he took employment with an American merchant named Henry Morton Stanley, and adopted his name. He fought with the rebel Confederate army during the American Civil War and was captured at the Battle of Shiloh in

1862. After the war he began his African explorations, at first as a correspondent for the *New York Herald*.

Stanley made six major trips to Africa, during which death was no stranger to his travels. Hundreds of his men perished of disease, starvation or violence. In his career as a journalist-explorer he accompanied the British punitive expedition in 1868 against the Ethiopian king, Theodore II; in 1871 he located the ailing Scottish missionary and explorer Dr David Livingston and together with him explored Lake Tanganyika; in 1873 he reported on the British campaign against the Ashanti in Ghana; from 1874 to 1877 he circumnavigated both Lakes Tanganyika and Victoria and crossed the continent from east to west, descending to the Atlantic Ocean along the Congo river. In 1879 he returned to the Congo for five years under the sponsorship of King Leopold of Belgium. In 1887 Stanley led an expedition to rescue the German explorer Emin Pasha, governor of Equatoria Province of the Egyptian Sudan, who was surrounded by rebellious Mahdist forces, but when he found Emin Pasha in 1888 he was unable to persuade him to return to Egypt. It was on this expedition that Stanley made a definite sighting of the Rwenzori. From 1895 to 1900 he sat in the British Parliament and was knighted in 1899.

Luigi Amedeo di Savoia, the Duke of Abruzzi (1873–1933) was born in Madrid to the then King of Spain, who abdicated his throne only a few weeks after his son's birth and returned to Italy. When he was six years old, young Luigi was assigned to the Italian Navy and received his entire education in military schools. A man of great energy and imagination, at the age of 24 he organised and led the expedition that

Luigi Amedeo di Savoia, the Duke of Abruzzi (centre), flanked by guides Joseph Petigax (left) and César Ollier. Taken on the 1906 Rwenzori expedition

Published with the permission of the Istituto di Fotografia Alpina 'Vittorio Sella'

made the first ascent of Mount St Elias (5,484 metres) in Alaska in 1897. Two years later he led an expedition to the North Pole which reached a latitude 86°34' north, a new record at the time. In 1906 he led the Rwenzori expedition which climbed all the major peaks and made the most extensive exploration of the range before or since. A few years later, in 1909, he organised an expedition to the Karakoram and set the record for the highest altitude yet achieved by ascending the second highest mountain in the world, K2, to a height of about 7,500 metres (24,600 feet), along the route that today bears his name, the Abruzzi Ridge. On the same journey he increased this record when he ascended Chogolisa (Bride Peak) to an even higher altitude, 7,654 metres (about 25,110 feet), but did not reach the summit. The first ascent to the summit of Chogolisa was not made until 45 years later.

During his great period of adventure and exploration, the Duke of Abruzzi remained a professional naval officer and

on 30 September 1911 he commanded the squadron that attacked Préveza, Greece, in the first action of the Italian–Turkish War. Later, he commanded the Adriatic fleet of the Italian navy in World War I and is warmly remembered in Italy for his heroic rescue of more than 100,000 Yugoslav refugees from Albania. In his last years he became interested in the exploration and agricultural development of Somalia and Ethiopia, eventually marrying a Somali wife. After several expeditions to the region and the establishment of various agricultural schemes, he died in Ethiopia on 18 March 1933, where he was buried. In the 1980s the Duke's family hoped to have his remains exhumed and returned to Italy, but bowed to the wishes of the Ethiopian villagers who refused to allow the exhumation, wanting to keep his remains – and memory – with them.

RWENZORI PEOPLE: THE BAKONZO

In large part, the people who inhabit the villages and farms immediately along the Uganda Rwenzori front hills are Bakonzo, commonly shortened to Konzo. Most trekkers in the Rwenzori hire the Bakonzo as guides and porters. They are generally slender, of medium height, and

Market acrobat

astonishingly strong in the mountains, capable of covering enormous distances in a few hours of intense walking.

In Uganda the Bakonzo are an important ethnic group of about 30,000 people and in Zaire they number more. Like mountain people around the world, they are industrious and self-reliant, able to pull back into the fastness of their hills in times of turmoil in the plains, which has rewarded them with a social stability rare in Uganda and Zaire over the last

Mountain farm

decades. The Bakonzo bear themselves with great dignity, are conscientious about education and have that wonderful core spirit of conservative African values and modest manners. They are relaxed and open. Humour is plentiful and a good joke can last for weeks.

The Bakonzo homesteads usually consist of only one or two rectangular houses and a few small store huts, widely scattered and perched on the ridges of the foothills. The houses are made of a double layer of plaited bamboo filled with clay and roofed with grass or banana thatch, although now more frequently with the ubiquitous African corrugated iron roof. Coffee (more recently some people grow cocoa) has been the main cash crop in the foothills. On the plains it is cotton. With an expanding population, recent economic policies favouring stability have taken hold, and farms are being pushed further and higher into the mountain foothills,

with the increasing potential for erosion and environmental damage caused by people pressure on the land.

The Bakonzo usually marry early, the girls at about 13 or 14. With increased educational and employment opportunities in recent years, and a stiff bride price, some men are now delaying marriage until they have established themselves in jobs or gained a small measure of prosperity. Polygamy is allowed, but constrained by economic resources or the church, although the latter does not weigh so heavily as the financial reality of supporting more than one wife and the children they bear. The climate is healthy, food and pure water are abundant; by comparison to other parts of Africa, survival birth-rates are high and the population is growing.

Agriculture is the principle occupation of the Bakonzo with a few recently having become cattle owners on a small scale. The men break the new ground, but the women manage the crop, climbing up the steep hillsides daily to plant, weed and hoe. The women bring goods to market, the men try to conjure up cash-earning businesses. Other than serving as porters for mountaineering groups going into the Rwenzori, employment opportunities for men are somewhat limited. A few might be plank-cutters, carpenters, blacksmiths or basket-makers, although it is not

Working the farm, high on Rwenzori slopes, looking over the Rift Valley into Zaire

Cotton is an important cash crop in the region

uncommon in the Rwenzori foothills to find that the skilled workers have actually come from towns further to the south due to restrictive land-tenure traditions in those regions, forcing them to seek work elsewhere. There are limited opportunities in store-keeping, local trading of cash crops and produced goods, butchery, and lately tourism, with the further development of hotels in the region. On the plains there is cotton growing, some fishing in the lakes, the cement plant at Hima and hope of future cash employment at the Kilembe copper mine above Kasese when it resumes production.

Despite the lack of regular cash employment, there is always portering, carrying loads up and down the steep mountain trails. The arrival, in the back of a pick-up truck, of a group of mountaineers winding their way up the dusty road from Kasese to Ibanda and beyond to Nyakalengija is met with cheers as they pass through the hamlets and banana groves. Jobs! Real money! The chance to meet some nice tourists who might take a few minutes over the course of a week to understand that the man carrying their rucksack is in fact a trainee accountant who pays his way by carrying loads for trekkers. Or perhaps he's a father of four children, all in school, for whom a small tip might double his real cash income for a month or more and pay the school fees for the next year.

RWENZORI NATIONAL PARK

Four-fifths of the Rwenzori range is in Uganda and only one-fifth in Zaire. The smaller Zairean portion has been protected as a National Park since the northward extension of Parc National d'Albert in 1929, and is now incorporated into Virunga National Park. By contrast, the Uganda Rwenzori had no statutory protection whatsoever until 1941, when all the terrain above 7,000 feet (about 2,200 metres) was made a central government Forest Reserve. This arrangement worked reasonably well until the general deterioration of government services in Uganda during the 1970s. It was not until the new government of President Yoweri Museveni came to power in 1986 that infrastructure and government services were revived. In that year, under the sponsorship of WWF International and the New York Zoological Society, Dr Peter Howard made a study of the range and presented a proposal for a National Park. At about the same time, Guy Yeoman, a British veterinary scientist working in East Africa, was conducting an extensive series of research trips into the range and waging a campaign for National Park status for the Rwenzori. As a result of his concentrated personal efforts and many publications, including his 1989 book, *Africa's Mountains of the Moon*, he was invited in 1990 by the European Community to outline a plan for a National Park. Finally, in May 1991, Rwenzori National Park was created. Some of Guy Yeoman's work was included in a submission made on behalf of the Ugandan government by Dr Derek Pomeroy and the professorial staff of the Environment Faculty at Makerere University which led to the designation of the Rwenzori as a United Nations World Heritage Site in 1994. This should help secure the further institutional strength and financial resources needed to protect the fragile environment.

The system of trails, huts and rock shelters in the Rwenzori was originally developed during the 1940s and 1950s by the Uganda Mountain Club with the construction of the Bujuku-Mubuku hut system. Recently two new huts have been added, John Matte Hut and Guy Yeoman Hut, a USAID contribution, and every season sees some further development of a small shelter, a park warden station or a bog-protecting (but rather unsightly) boardwalk.

Political stability in Uganda, a worldwide increase in tourist travel and National Park status for the Rwenzori has resulted in more tourists visiting the range. Whereas in the past there might have been 200 to 300 visitors per year to the range, now there are 1,000 or more per year, each accompanied by at least one guide or porter and usually more. The increase in traffic has had serious impact on the fragile vegetation along the most heavily travelled tourist routes. The dilemma is that fee-paying tourists are needed to support the conservation work in the park, while at the same time they increase the environmental damage. The policies and actions needed to mitigate this problem are complex and expensive. Visitors should be aware that the park fees they pay, no matter how high, cover only a small portion of the budget needed to protect the Rwenzori.

THE PHOTOGRAPHS OF VITTORIO SELLA

This book contains several black and white photographs, including a fold-out panorama of the Rwenzori range, printed from the original negatives of Vittorio Sella (1859–1943), the Italian alpinist and photographer who accompanied the 1906 Abruzzi Rwenzori expedition and who was perhaps the greatest of all alpine photographers. It was Sella who first recorded the landscape, plants and people of the Rwenzori in extensive and intimate detail, and to whom we refer for clarity of the historical record and pure artistic beauty. It is particularly interesting to note how far the glaciers of the Rwenzori have

Vittorio Sella and friend

Published with the permission of the Istituto di "Fotografia Alpina 'Vittorio Sella'

receded since these photographs were taken, nearly 90 years ago.

Vittorio Sella was born in Biella, Italy, to a father who was a successful textile industrialist and scientist and who, in 1856, had been the first Italian to write a treatise on photography. Vittorio owed his interest in the mountains to his uncle, Quintino, founder of the Alpine Club of Italy. As a young man, Vittorio had worked as a chemist in his father's textile factory, but it was his passion for taking beautiful panoramic photographs of the mountains which made him famous. From 1880 to 1893 he compiled a detailed portfolio of the Alps, combining his photography with impressive alpinism, such as the first winter traverse of the Matterhorn in 1882. He made three expeditions to the Caucasus, in 1889, 1890 and 1896, for which his photography received awards from Britain's Royal Geographical Society. In 1899 he accompanied his friend the alpinist D.W. Freshfield on a difficult exploration of Kanchenjunga in Sikkim. The Duke of Abruzzi greatly admired Sella's work and invited him to be the official photographer for the expeditions in 1897 to Mount St Elias in Alaska, in 1906 to the Rwenzori and in 1909 to the Karakoram. The highest summit on Mount Luigi di Savoia in the Rwenzori was named Sella Peak in his honour.

David Pluth

THE JOURNEY

THIS COLLECTION OF photographs of the Uganda Rwenzori mountains covers the range from the north near Bundibugyo on the west side of the mountains, around the northern hills and south along the eastern foothills to Queen Elizabeth National Park, with incursions into the centre of the range. The photographs are arranged in the order and style of a journey through the mountains and villages.

The photographs start in Fort Portal, one of the access points, along with the railhead of Kasese, to the Rwenzori from Kampala. After a circuit of the Rwenzori, the trip takes us into the surrounding villages and countryside.

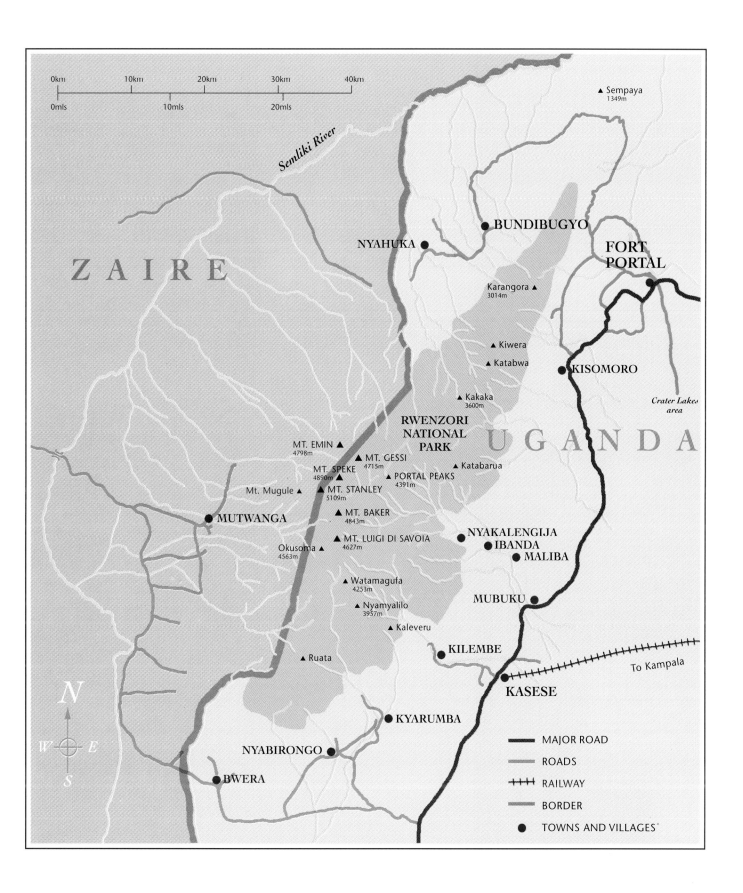

0km 10km 20km 30km 40km

0mls 10mls 20mls

Semliki River

Z A I R E

▲ Sempaya
1349m

● BUNDIBUGYO

NYAHUKA ●

FORT
PORTAL

Karangora ▲
3014m

● KISOMORO

▲ Kiwera

▲ Katabwa

*Crater Lakes
area*

▲ Kakaka
3600m

RWENZORI
NATIONAL
PARK

U G A N D A

MT. EMIN ▲
4798m

▲ MT. GESSI
4715m

▲ Katabarua

MT. SPEKE
4890m ▲

▲ PORTAL PEAKS
4391m

Mt. Mugule ▲

▲ MT. STANLEY
5109m

▲ MT. BAKER
4843m

● MUTWANGA

▲ MT. LUIGI DI SAVOIA
4627m

● NYAKALENGIJA

Okusoma ▲
4563m

● IBANDA

● MALIBA

▲ Watamagufa
4253m

● MUBUKU

▲ Nyamyalilo
3957m

▲ Kaleveru

● KILEMBE

To Kampala

▲ Ruata

● KASESE

N

● KYARUMBA

W ✦ E

S

● NYABIRONGO

MAJOR ROAD

● BWERA

ROADS

RAILWAY

BORDER

● TOWNS AND VILLAGES

FORT PORTAL

FORT PORTAL IS an attractive community at the north-eastern end of the Rwenzori near the brink of the steep escarpment plunging 700 metres down to the floor of the Western Rift Valley. The town, surrounded by large tea estates and banana groves, is the centre of the Toro District and the Toro Kingdom, which was established in the early nineteenth century by a rebel Banyoro prince called Kaboyo. On a hilltop overlooking the town are the houses and the large building which comprise the palace of the king of Toro.

House on Kiamara tea estate near Fort Portal

FACING PAGE
Buzirasagama Tea Estate near Fort Portal
has been operating for more than 90 years

Tea is everywhere in Fort Portal

Building a church on the Toro tea estates near Fort Portal. Religion, both Christianity and Islam, plays a large part in the lives of the people

FACING PAGE
Wood transporter in Fort Portal

Young acrobat on a tea shamba near Fort Portal

FACING PAGE
Morning over the tea gardens in Fort Portal

Fort Portal market

Young boy on a tea shamba near
Fort Portal

Local accommodation, Fort Portal

Development is in progress in the Rwenzori foothills.
The road from Kampala to Fort Portal is being improved every year,
as are roads throughout Uganda

Rwenzori cloud walker

FACING PAGE
Storm brewing over the tea gardens, Fort Portal

Fort Portal morning glory

Fort Portal lily, kniphofia

John Simpson, Uganda tea planter
since 1956

Tea tasting

Rwenzori Commodities

THE RWENZORI MOUNTAINS

MOST PEOPLE ARRIVE in the Rwenzori by road from Kampala to either Fort Portal or Kasese, or by train to Kasese. Then they wind their way along the paved highway, perhaps passing the cement plant at Hima if coming from Fort Portal, through the cotton fields, turning west next to the electrical power substation at the sign that says Rwenzori National Park. From the highway there is a dusty 15 kilometre track to Nyakalengija where trekkers check in with park headquarters, pay their park entrance and rescue fees and buy last minute groceries. Here they meet their Bakonzo guides and porters who quickly organise things, weigh the baggage and divide it into loads. In short order everything is ready to go. Some people choose to stay an extra night at Nyakalengija, hoping for an early morning start the next day, others march on without pause, hoping to make it to the first hut before the afternoon rains.

Most trekkers make a five- to seven-day journey around a circuit in the central Rwenzori, visiting most of the major peaks and reaching altitudes of over 4,200 metres. The conditions, even for experienced trekkers, can be challenging, with steep slippery trails, deep mud, tussock bogs, heavy rain, snow, cold and river crossings. The mountains are more remote than they seem at first. In an emergency rescue is not easy; the victim may need to be carried out by porters.

Rwenzori National Park entrance

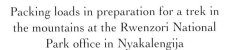

Packing loads in preparation for a trek in the mountains at the Rwenzori National Park office in Nyakalengija

FACING PAGE
Morning at the Rwenzori National Park headquarters at Nyakalengija

Nyabitaba

DEPARTING FROM THE park headquarters at Nyakalengija, the trip begins with a short walk through the village of typical Bakonzo homes and gradually climbs through elephant grass, garden plots and finally open grassy pastures where Friesian cattle graze. On reaching the national park boundary, it may be possible to buy a warm soft drink from an enterprising park warden. The trail then follows the Mubuku river for about two and a half hours, through landslide areas and up and down over rocks and bluffs before reaching the Mahoma river. After crossing the river the trail starts to climb steeply through bracken fern slopes and podocarpus forest to Nyabitaba Hut on a forested ridge at about 2,650 metres (8,700 feet). On the upward climb you may hear chimpanzees or spot colobus or blue monkeys and catch glimpses of the brilliant tree-top bird, the Rwenzori turacao. It is not uncommon to see giant earthworms on this trail, 30–45 centimetres long (12–18 inches) and as thick as an index finger. Across the valley from Nyabitaba Hut the Portal Peaks can be seen, often glowing with shades of blue in the evening and warm reds in the morning light.

Small farms are passed shortly after leaving Nyakalengija

Giant banana leaves arch over the
trail in the park

Approaching the National Park boundary
about one hour from Nyakalengija.
Friesian cattle have been introduced

Rain and hail at Nyabitaba Hut

Arriving at Nyabitaba Hut

FACING PAGE
The Portal Peaks can be seen from
Nyabitaba

Morning over the Portal Peaks from Nyakalengija

Then and now.

Porters from the 1906 Duke of Abuzzi expedition ...

Published with the permission of the Istituto di Fotografia Alpina 'Vittorio Sella'

... and a modern crew 90 years later

John Matte Hut

THE TRAIL DROPS down from Nyabitaba Hut to the Kurt Shafer Bridge crossing just below the confluence of the Bujuku and Mubuku rivers. This important bridge, which greatly reduces the danger of crossing the river, was a USAID project. After the bridge, the trail starts a steep ascent through bamboo forest, traversing a long and exhausting stretch of slippery rock slide. If it is raining, this section of trail will be memorable. After about five hours the old hut and rock shelter of Nyamileju is reached. The name means 'place of beards', a reference to the lichen and moss which drapes the trees. From here, on clear days, Mounts Stanley and Speke can be seen. Nyamileju is also the start of the giant heather, lobelia and groundsel zone, the remarkable vegetation found only on high-altitude African mountains. The final two-hour walk to John Matte (also spelt Mate) Hut at about 3,400 metres (11,200 feet) is through a tiring bog, climbing over the roots of the extraordinary plants, offering an opportunity to become intimately acquainted with the vegetation.

Porters' huts at John Matte camp

Starting up the Bujuku valley

'The very air seemed tinged in an eerie green light'

Eric Shipton, *Upon that Mountain*

First glimpse of the peaks at the head of the Bujuku valley

FACING PAGE
Shortly after descending from Nyabitaba Hut, the Mubuku river is crossed below its
confluence with the Bujuku river on the Kurt Shafer Bridge, a USAID project

Drying out at John Matte Hut

Helichrysum near John Matte Hut

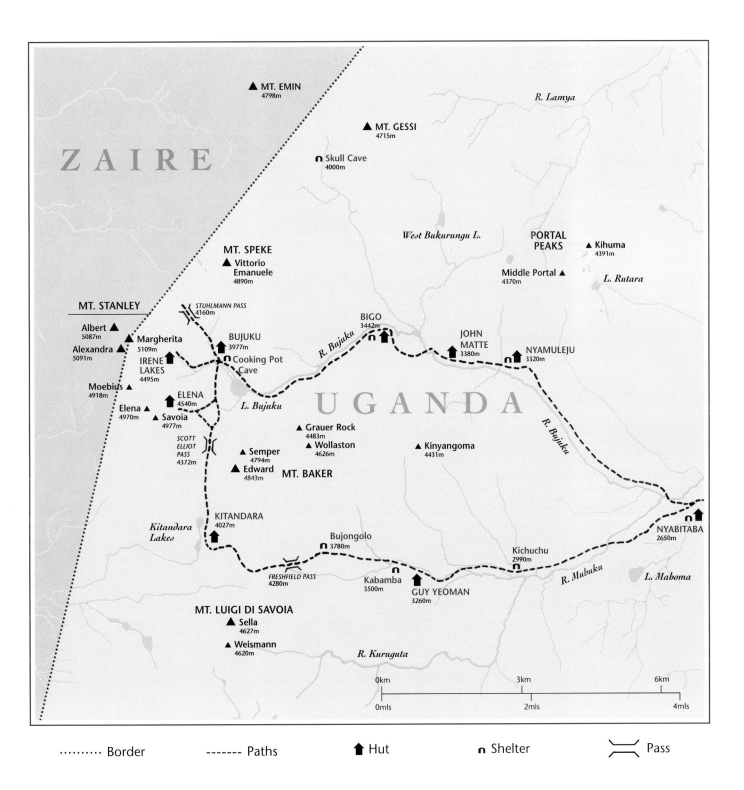

▲ MT. EMIN
4798m

R. Lamya

▲ MT. GESSI
4715m

∩ Skull Cave
4000m

West Bukurungu L.

PORTAL
PEAKS

▲ Kihuma
4391m

Z A I R E

MT. SPEKE

▲ Vittorio
Emanuele
4890m

Middle Portal ▲
4370m

L. Rutara

MT. STANLEY

STUHLMANN PASS
4160m

BIGO
3442m

JOHN
MATTE
3380m

Albert ▲
5087m

▲ Margherita
5109m

BUJUKU
3977m

∩ ⬆

NYAMULEJU
3320m

Alexandra ▲
5091m

IRENE
LAKES
4495m

⬆ Cooking Pot
Cave

R. Bujuku

⬆

Moebius ▲
4918m

ELENA
4540m

⬆

U G A N D A

R. Bujuku

Elena ▲
4970m

▲ Savoia
4977m

L. Bujuku

*SCOTT
ELLIOT
PASS*
4372m

▲ Grauer Rock
4483m

▲ Semper
4794m

▲ Wollaston
4626m

▲ Kinyangoma
4431m

▲ Edward
4843m

MT. BAKER

KITANDARA
4027m

⬆

Bujongolo
∩ 3780m

Kichuchu
2990m

NYABITABA
2650m

*Kitandara
Lakes*

FRESHFIELD PASS
4280m

Kabamba
3500m

⬆
GUY YEOMAN
3260m

R. Mubuku

L. Mahoma

MT. LUIGI DI SAVOIA

▲ Sella
4627m

▲ Weismann
4620m

R. Kuruguta

0km   3km   6km

0mls   2mls   4mls

·········· Border   ------- Paths   ⬆ Hut   ∩ Shelter   ⟩⟨ Pass

Morning breaks over the hills at
John Matte camp

The Portal Peaks from John Matte Hut

FACING PAGE
Mount Speke is glimpsed in the morning
light just before entering Lower Bigo Bog

On the edge of Lower Bigo Bog giant heather trees are draped with old man's beard (usnea)

FACING PAGE
Mount Speke from the tussocks in Lower Bigo Bog – the passage of trekkers has flattened
the tussock tops and turned the ground between into mud

Bujuku

FROM JOHN MATTE Hut the trail crosses the Bujuku river and enters Lower Bigo Bog; this is the start of the game of tussock-jumping, springing from head to head, in an attempt – usually in vain – to avoid the mud below. This can be particularly exhilarating on a frosty morning, much like jumping on giant ice cubes floating in frozen mud. There has been some recent work to build boardwalks along the section of trail skirting Lower Bigo Bog in an effort to reduce the impact of the many tourists visiting the mountains. At the end of Lower Bigo Bog there is a steep climb to Upper Bigo Bog, where the trail is partly covered with an older boardwalk. While the boardwalk may be an eyesore, it keeps hikers from widening the area of damaged tussocks and churned-up mud. From Upper Bigo Bog the trail climbs for about an hour and a half to Lake Bujuku with, on the rare clear days, fabulous views of Mount Baker to the south and Mount Stanley to the west. The trail along the north edge of the lake is simply deep mud. In *Snow on the Equator*, H.W. Tilman wrote, 'It was not quicksand, but a very fair imitation. We began floundering along the margin of the lake, sinking to our knees in the noisome mud at every step. We … resigned ourselves to long wallowing in the slough.' Beyond the lake at about 3,960 metres (13,000 feet) is Bujuku Hut, favourably located for climbing Mounts Baker and Speke, in a narrow valley below Stuhlmann Pass and between Mount Stanley and Mount Speke; but the sun sets early and, even for the Rwenzori, the nights can be cold.

View across Lower Bigo Bog towards Mount Gessi

Giant lobelia

*'La poesia di questa natura non si comprende e
non si sente, trovandosi al di là della vita'*
(I am unable to fully understand or
appreciate the poetry of this landscape, as there
is in it no sign of animal life)

Vittorio Sella, quoted from his Rwenzori
diaries

Published with the permission of the Istituto di Fotografia Alpina 'Vittorio Sella'

Lobelia rosette in Lower Bigo Bog

A glimpse of Mount Speke in the clouds above Upper Bigo Bog

FACING PAGE
Everlasting flowers starting to open in the sun, Lower Bigo Bog

A moment of colour crossing the Bujuku river in Upper Bigo Bog

FACING PAGE
View north-east across the Upper Bigo Bog. Note the boardwalk trail slicing through the valley –
it may not be attractive, but it probably saves the delicate vegetation

Vegetation in the forest bordering Lower Bigo Bog

FACING PAGE
Moss in the forest near Bigo Bog

Lake Bujuku and the lower flanks of Mount Baker

Mount Baker and Scott Elliot Pass

Giant groundsels and Mount Baker

'Our eyes lingered on the grim precipices across the valley below the snows of Mount Baker, on the serrated ridge of the Scott Elliot Pass and the peaks and glaciers of Mount Stanley. This was a view seldom, if ever, seen in whole … we were usually compelled to trust to fleeting glimpses of rock and ice, peak and ridge, seen through the writhing mists, and in imagination link the whole together'

H.W. Tilman, *Snow on the Equator*

Lake Bujuku mud and rain

'It was not quicksand, but a very fair imitation. We began floundering along the margin of the lake, sinking to our knees in the noisome mud at every step. We … resigned ourselves to long wallowing in the slough'

H.W. Tilman, *Snow on the Equator*

Mount Speke clouds

Glacial lakes on the west side of Mount Speke

Footprints in the frozen mud of Lake Bujuku

In the fog on Mount Speke. The Duke of Abruzzi *'attempted to proceed but was very soon forced to return, the fog being so dense it seemed like night'*

Fillipo de Fillipi, *Ruwenzori*

FACING PAGE
Bujuku camp at the foot of Mount Speke

Mount Stanley reflected in the icy water
of Lake Bujuku on a cold morning

Vincent dressed in red at Bujuku

Porters cooking at Bujuku Hut

Mount Stanley and Lake Bujuku

Published with the permission of the Istituto di Fotografia Alpina 'Vittorio Sella'

Scott Elliot Pass and Elena Hut

THE TRAIL CONTINUES directly west from Bujuku Hut and climbs the slopes to the west of the lake, passing through the magical Groundsel Gully as it ascends to Scott Elliot Pass at 4,372 metres (14,345 feet). At the head of the gully a short metal ladder lies over a particularly steep section, after which the trail branches, the right fork leading up to Elena Hut and Mount Stanley over a steep rocky track, the left fork leading to Scott Elliot Pass and down to the Kitandara Lakes. The small Elena Hut (4,540 metres, 14,895 feet) sits in the rocks at the base of the Stanley Glacier, roughly a three-hour walk (depending on the weather conditions and the climber's acclimatisation) from the summit of Margherita Peak.

Margherita Peak, 1906
Published with the permission of the Istituto di Fotografia Alpina 'Vittorio Sella'

Alexandra Peak from Margherita Peak

'At last a clearing came. It lasted hardly a minute,
but it was long enough for us to see and recognise the familiar summit of Alexandra,
and to realise that we must be on Margherita. It was sheer luck …'

H.W. Tilman, *Snow on the Equator*

Groundsels in the mists

Lichens and moss on a rock at 4,400
metres (about 14,500 feet)

Ladder on one of the steep sections leading to Scott Elliot Pass
and Elena Hut

Elena Hut has a grim aspect on a
cloudy day

Waiting out the weather at Elena Hut

Two climbers on the Stanley glacier, 1906
(Alexandra Peak on the left, Margherita Peak on the right)

Published with the permission of the Istituto di Fotografia Alpina 'Vittorio Sella'

Kitandara, Freshfield Pass and Mount Baker

FROM THE PASS there are spectacular views back to Bujuku Hut and Mount Speke, up to Mount Stanley and down the valley to the Kitandara Lakes. Once over Scott Elliot Pass the trail enters an alpine zone of sparse low vegetation and stark rough boulders along the massive rock walls of Mount Baker. After passing through the impact craters of huge

boulders careening down the slopes of Mount Baker, and bad mud at the bottom of the valley, the day ends at the lower Kitandara Lake, at about 4,020 metres (13,200 feet). As at Bujuku Hut, the sun sets early here and the nights can be cold.

From Kitandara the trail again ascends steeply (as usual) up the headwall spreading out from the base of Mount

Baker and continues along the south side of the mountain to Freshfield Pass. On a clear day there are views westward into the Rift Valley of Zaire and northward to Mount Stanley. Freshfield Pass is a long, nearly flat traverse through beautiful high alpine glades – and mud – until, on the far side of the pass, the trail begins its long two-day descent.

Savoia Peak (4,977 metres) on Mount Stanley from Freshfield Pass

Kitandara Lake and hut – McConnell's Prong on Mount Luigi di Savoia
is visible in the background

FACING PAGE
Crossing a stream near the Kitandara Lakes

Evening clouds drift in from Zaire between Mount Stanley (on the right)
and Mount Luigi di Savoia

FACING PAGE
Colours on Freshfield Pass can seem unreal

Evening on the twin summits of Mount Stanley,
looking across the remnants of Mount Baker's Edward Glacier

Mount Stanley from Baker's summit
*'The whole scene stood revealed, and took on a fresh aspect
in this almost unnatural sunlight'*
H.W. Tilman, *Snow on the Equator*

Mount Speke from Mount Baker

Julius Mate enjoys the sunshine on the
summit of Mount Baker

Colours at our feet, descending Baker to Freshfield Pass

Moss bordering an alpine tarn on Mount Baker

Small scenes emerge even on grey days

The vegetation is being worn away and churned into mud on the descent from Freshfield Pass to Guy Yeoman Hut

Colours at the crossing, Freshfield Pass

Guy Yeoman Hut and Return

THE ROUTE DOWN to Guy Yeoman Hut at 3,260 metres (10,700 feet) passes the rock shelter at Bujongolo, the base camp for the 1906 Duke of Abruzzi expedition. From Guy Yeoman Hut it is possible to reach the park headquarters at Nyakalengija in one day, but this would be a fairly long day for most people. The path down from Guy Yeoman can be treacherous in spots, the heavy trekker traffic having stripped away the supporting vegetation to expose pure vertical mud or steep rock with few handholds. The Bakonzo porters will, of course, prance over this ground like angels, but most trekkers at this point will be trying their best not to slide down the rocks and to stay afloat on the bogs.

Peaks at the head of the Mubuku valley

*'As if by magic, the snow-clad ranges loom into sight only
to vanish again and leave the onlooker in doubt and uncertainty
as to the actual reality of the magnificent vision'*

Fillipo de Fillipi, *Ruwenzori*

Patterns on the valley wall

Moss on a Mubuku river rock

Giant heathers silhouetted in the glow of evening light near Guy Yeoman Hut

Mubuku river near Kabamba

FACING PAGE
Vertical green in the upper Mubuku valley

THE ROAD NORTH – BUNDIBUGYO

BUNDIBUGYO IS ON the west side of the mountains near the Semliki river and the Ugandan border with Zaire. It is reached by travelling around the north end of the Rwenzori along the Semliki road, one of the most spectacular road trips in East Africa. From Fort Portal the road is cut into the side of the mountains above the rift valley and then, after crossing the northern spine of the mountains, plunges down to the Semliki river. Once a prosperous trading town for cocoa and coffee, Bundibugyo is still rebuilding itself after the economic decline of the 1970s and early 1980s. Cocoa, in particular, is making a comeback.

Bundibugyo is the site of a large market and a Pygmy re-settlement project; it has more of a central African feeling than most towns in western Uganda, perhaps due to its proximity to Zaire and relatively few visitors.

The last valley, rounding the northern end of the Rwenzori on the Semliki road

The Semliki road to Bundibugyo winds through mountain farms
at the northern end of the Rwenzori

Houses perched on a Rwenzori ridge
overlooking the Rift Valley in Zaire

Young girl scraping at the steep slopes of
the family farm above Bundibugyo

Pounding cassava high up on a mountain
farm near Bundibugyo

FACING PAGE
Mother pauses from planting

Green coffee beans, future cash
on the vine

Donkeys carrying water in Nyahuka,
near Bundibugyo

Nyahuka Holiday Inn

Clothes and cocoa beans drying in the
sun near Bundibugyo

Village house in Bundibugyo

Rainbow mist rises over a farmer's house near Bundibugyo

Matooke (plantains), cooking pot and drying cassava; looking south along the Zairean side of the Rwenzori

Woman in doorway

Young mother and child, Bundibugyo

Main street in Bundibugyo on market day

Car Park Hotel and Richard, the proprietor, Bundibugyo

THE CRATER LAKES

IN THE HILLS about 30 kilometres south of Fort Portal lies a necklace of sparkling gems: the 25 Bunyuruguru volcanic crater lakes, each one a different shade of blue or green. Local legends claim the lakes were made by the first Bachwezi king, Ndahura, when he retired to the area after abdicating in favour of his son Wamara. This is beautiful walking country, with gentle hills, open paths and spectacular views of the Rwenzori mountains to the west. The scenic charm of the area was remarked upon by many of the early explorers to the range who approached overland from Kampala, and the region is today experiencing strong growth in tourist development.

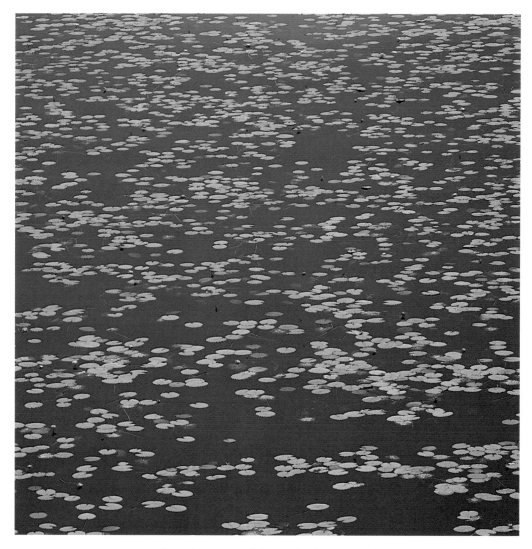

Lily pads on crater lake south of Fort Portal

FACING PAGE
Nyambuga crater lake south of Fort Portal

Grass near crater lake shore

FACING PAGE
View across the volcanic foothills south of Fort Portal to the
mass of the Rwenzori

*'My eyes were directed by a boy to a mountain, said to be covered with salt,
and I saw a peculiar shaped cloud … which assumed the proportions and
appearance of a vast mountain covered with snow. Following its form
downward … I became for the first time conscious that what I gazed upon
was not the image or semblance of a vast mountain, but the solid
substance of a real one, with its summit covered with snow … It now
dawned upon me that this must be the Ruwenzori …'*

Henry Stanley, *In Darkest Africa*

Nyambuga crater lake at dawn, from Ndali Lodge

FACING PAGE
Looking south from Ndali Lodge across the Mwamba crater lake
towards Kasese with the Rwenzori rising on the right

Bicycles bringing *matooke* from the foothills to the market in Fort Portal

A growing economy needs bricks, but it takes firewood to make them. Brick-making perhaps best symbolises the difficult choices between economic development and environmental protection

Bricks drying

Bricks provide employment for all ages –
young boys stack bricks for sale

Achole cattle

FACING PAGE
Rwenzori cattle with herder

MUBUKU VALLEY VILLAGES AND THE FOOTHILLS

THE MUBUKU VALLEY has been the traditional eastern approach to the Rwenzori range. This heavily populated and cultivated area is filled with small mountain farms, villages and markets which, even though so close to the normal tourist routes, are seldom visited.

However, some of the best views of the mountains (other than from the summits of the highest peaks themselves) can be had from these comparatively low foothills only a few kilometres from the main Fort Portal–Kasese highway. Just wandering in the hills, visiting the

markets and talking to the friendly, open people can be fascinating. The normal food crops of cassava and bananas (*matooke*) are grown, together with cash crops of coffee, some cocoa and, more recently, passion fruit.

View up the Mubuku valley towards Mount Baker near Kyanya

Hilltop village overlooking the
Mubuku valley

Mount Stanley seen from Bweyale.
Mount Baker is on the left, the snows of
Mount Speke on the right just visible
behind the grey mass of the Portal Peaks

Salt seller, Maliba market

Serious young cloth merchant in
Maliba market

Boy carrying sugar cane

The Bakonzo women *'never come as expedition porters, although they could do just as well as their men, so sturdily do they carry loads up and down the foothill paths. Massive stems of the great green cooking plantains, jars and jerry cans of beer or water, and large, finely plaited baskets of food crops and flour are transported only by the women – all this and baby too!'*

Guy Yeoman, *Africa's Mountains of the Moon*

Re-wrapping on the way to a mountain market

FACING PAGE
Mountain farms above the Mubuku valley

Maliba market pilgrims

Drums as churchbells – calling the congregation to church in Kangwangi, Buhunga Parish, above the Mubuku valley

Mother, firewood and baby on the way home

Storm approaching in the foothills

Coffee beans

Spreading coffee beans to dry in the
Mubuku valley

Making lumber from logs near Buhunga

Wet freshly-sawn wood, the result of a
long day's work

FACING PAGE
Matooke section of Maliba market

KASESE AND THE SOUTHERN RWENZORI

KASESE IS THE railhead of the line between Kampala and western Uganda. It is the largest town near the Rwenzori, serving as a regional trading centre, and is the home of some of the largest industries in the country.

The Hima cement factory is to the north of Kasese, and to the west, directly up one of the Rwenzori valleys is Kilembe Mine. This copper and cobalt mine is currently undergoing renovation and will provide cash employment once it is fully operational again. The fertile land near Kasese also supports large cotton plantations as well as the traditional food crops.

To the south of Kasese the Rwenzori gradually diminish in height, finally levelling out into the plains of Queen Elizabeth National Park. The foothills in the south are fertile and heavily cultivated. This area is seldom visited by tourists, who are more intent on the traditional approaches, but the villages lie in spectacular valley settings which could easily be starting points for lengthy traverses of the range. Queen Elizabeth National Park is Uganda's most famous park, happily now enjoying a recovery in its wildlife population which was decimated by hunting during the 1970s and 1980s.

Kasese main street

Cloth seller in Kasese market

The Saad Hotel, a Kasese landmark for Rwenzori travellers

Cosy Photographic Studio, Kasese

Barbecuing chickens on the street in Kasese

Schoolhouse in Kilembe

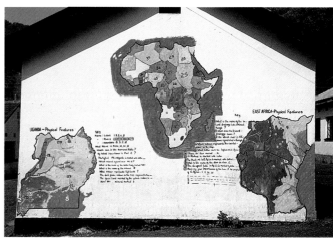

FACING PAGE
The Hima cement plant is another example of the
potential for conflicts between economic development,
jobs and the environment

Cotton is an important cash crop in the region

The copper and cobalt mine at Kilembe will be renovated and put back into production, providing much-needed cash employment in the region

Storm brewing over Kazinga Channel in Queen Elizabeth National Park to the south of the Rwenzori. In the centre of the picture is a herd of water buffalo

The southern Rwenzori, looking north across the grass plains from Queen Elizabeth National Park

Plants in Queen Elizabeth National Park

Stores and storage houses, Kyarumba

Nandi flame tree in the southern Rwenzori foothills

FACING PAGE
Farms in the foothills south of the Rwenzori

Bicycle pride

Boy selling peppers

Women carrying wood in the southern
Rwenzori hills

Open doors to the future – house and small shop decorated with map of Uganda

FURTHER READING

The following selected books and articles are suggested for those who wish to learn more about the Rwenzori range, particularly its history.

Rennie M. Bere
The Way to the Mountains of the Moon
Arthur Barker, 1966
An entertaining book by a former director and chief warden of the Uganda National Parks with exhaustive knowledge of the Rwenzori.

Douglas Busk
The Fountains of the Sun
Max Parrish, 1957
A diplomat-mountaineer relates his adventures in Ethiopia and the Rwenzori.

Fillipo de Fillipi
Ruwenzori, an account of the expedition of H.R.H. Prince Luigi Amedeo of Savoy, Duke of the Abruzzi
Archibald Constable, Dutton, 1908
The official account of the definitive expedition to the Rwenzori in 1906, with magnificent fold-out panoramas and photographs by Vittorio Sella. All the major peaks were climbed. The classic reference work to the range.

D.W. Freshfield
'Ruwenzori', **Alpine Journal** (1906), 23, 172: 87–98, 175: 310–313

D.W. Freshfield
'Towards Ruwenzori', **Alpine Journal** (1907), 23, 172: 87–98, 173: 185–202

G. Noel Humphries
'Ruwenzori', **Alpine Journal** (1927), 39, 234: 99–104

G. Noel Humphries
'New Routes on Ruwenzori', **Geographical Journal** (1927), 69, 516–531

G. Noel Humphries
'Ruwenzori: flights and further explorations', **Geographical Journal** (1933), 82, 481–514

Paul Joynson-Hicks
Uganda, The Pearl of Africa
Quiller Press, 1994
Beautiful photographs taken throughout Uganda by a resident artist.

Charles Miller
The Lunatic Express
The MacMillan Company, 1971
Building the railroad that brought the explorers, adventurers and tourists to Uganda.

J.E.S. Moore
To the Mountains of the Moon
Hurst & Blackett, 1901
An early expedition to the range. The party ascended the Mubuku valley to Bujongolo, base camp for the 1906 Duke of Abruzzi expedition, and climbed to the main ridge of Mount Baker by the East Baker Glacier in March 1900.

Alan Moorehead
The White Nile
Hamish Hamilton, 1960
An entertaining popular account of the history of the exploration of the Nile, which first brought Europeans into contact with the mountains of east and central Africa.

H.A. Osmaston and D. Pasteur
Guide to the Ruwenzori: The Mountains of the Moon
Mountain Club of Uganda and West Col Productions, UK, 1972
The only real climbing guide to the Rwenzori range. Includes a bibliography of the range up to 1968. Hopefully, this excellent guide will be republished.

D. Pasteur
'An expedition to the Emin and Gessi areas on Ruwenzori', **Alpine Journal** (1964), 69, 309: 191–200.

G.F. Scott Elliot
A Naturalist in mid-Africa: being an account of a journey to the Mountains of the Moon and Tanganyika
A.D. Innes, 1896
Written by one of the earliest explorers to the central Rwenzori, after whom Scott Elliot Pass is named.

Eric Shipton
Upon that Mountain
Hodder & Stoughton, 1943
Early autobiography of a great mountaineer and explorer. With Tilman, he made the third ascent of Mount Stanley.

Henry Morton Stanley,
In Darkest Africa or the Quest, Rescue and Retreat of Emin, Governor of Equatoria
Sampson Low, Marston, Searle & Rivington, 1890
The first definite sighting of the Rwenzori by European explorers and an account of the first attempt to climb one of the snow peaks. Emotive Victorian writing style.

Patrick M. Synge
Mountains of the Moon
Drummond, 1937
A British Museum expedition to study the flora and fauna. Includes accounts of the Rwenzori, Mount Kenya, Mount Elgon, the Virunga and Aberdare mountains.

H.W. Tilman
Snow on the Equator
Bell, 1937
Two planters in Kenya, Tilman and Shipton, tackle the mountains at their doorstep. Forerunner to the many later expeditions of these two famous adventurers and early Everest climbers.

Carveth Wells
In Coldest Africa
Robert M McBride & Company, 1929
Zany. Freezing on Mount Baker, 'Africa's Equatorial Arctic', following in the footsteps of the Duke of Abruzzi.

Andrew Wielochowski
Ruwenzori Map and Guide
West Col, 1989
Recommended to carry in the mountains. Best available information in a concise form.

A.F.R. Wollaston
From Ruwenzori to the Congo
Murray, 1908
Mountaineer-naturalist's account of his travels and work in Africa.

Guy Yeoman
Africa's Mountains of the Moon: Journeys to the Snowy Sources of the Nile
Hamish Hamilton; Universe Books, 1989
The last real adventures in the Rwenzori by the man who pushed for sensible development of the National Park. Good descriptions of the Bakonzo people. Informative, enjoyable, and a useful bibliography.